CONTENTS

FEAR OF FLYING?

WIN AEROPHOBIA IN A NATURAL WAY BY OVERCOMING ALL ANXIETY

Dr. Gabriele Buracchi Psychobiologist

PREFACE

During my professional activity mainly carried out in the field of nutrition and so-called eating disorders, I have however had the opportunity to meet people with anxiety disorders.

Among these, some people who specifically complained of the fear of flying, also known as Aerophobia, proved to be of particular interest.

These patients were therefore an opportunity for me to delve deeper into these problems in theory and also in practice, which are extremely engaging for the people affected but also for those who find themselves interacting with them.

This book was born precisely from these professional experiences and the techniques discussed in the second part of the book to help people solve these problems were the ones I usually used successfully with my patients.

I hope this book can be useful to many.

FEAR OF FLYING
OR AEROPHOBIA

Fear of flying (FoF) is a very widespread phenomenon both among those who habitually use airplanes as a means of transport and among those who have never flown.

This fear can manifest itself at any moment of a flight, whether short or long, business or leisure, planned or improvised, calm or turbulent.

If all phases of flight can be experienced with fear, some are certainly the most feared, such as take-off and landing.

The weather conditions that most frequently arouse anxiety are primarily turbulence, followed by thunderstorms, fog and strong winds.

The intensity of the fear experienced can manifest itself in different ways, varying depending on the person.

It can range from the simple discomfort felt before or during the flight, therefore a manifestation that is still controllable and which does not create particular limitations, up to the absolute terror that prevents one from tackling the flight.

In this case the discomforts are very serious and can range from acute anxiety crises to real panic attacks [1], with possible somatic manifestations.

FoF is often felt even by those who have never flown, blocking the person right from the simple decision to take the plane.

When we want to establish the origin and cause of various mental disorders, we move within the framework of various hypotheses.

The biological and psychological hypotheses have always faced alternating events; currently the dominant hypothesis integrates both mechanisms and is therefore considered the most complete, although, naturally, not all mental disorders can be considered equivalent.

For more information on anxiety disorders you can read: ANSIA. ATTACCHI DI PANICO, FOBIE, COMPULSIONI, OSSESSIONI, DISTURBO POST TRAUMATICO DA STRESS, FAME NERVOSA. COSA SONO E COME SI GUARISCE IN MODO NATURALE [2]

IS FOF A SPECIFIC DISORDER OR IS IT PART OF A MORE GENERAL ANXIETY PICTURE?

Aerophobia - or FoF - is classified among anxiety disorders and is among the so-called specific phobias, the most widespread forms of anxiety today.

The symptoms of FoF present various nuances that give rise to extensive overlaps with other anxiety disorders.

It is therefore not possible to separate FoF from anxiety disorders in general.

It is very rare, in fact, for FoF to present itself in isolation; more often it is associated with other types of phobias, especially those for means of transport, heights and closed places.

These specific phobias manifest themselves as an unreasonable fear, without apparent justification, marked and persistent, of a specific object, place or situation.

The person who suffers from it is usually fully aware of the irrationality of his fear, yet he is completely victim of it.

Often the person affected by FoF very strongly "*justifies*" this phobia with the need for rational control:

"I ONLY GET ON A PLANE IF I DRIVE IT"

A statement of this type highlights the constitution of a self-referred reality , in which all events are traced back to themselves, highlighting, as we have already mentioned, the existence of a more general anxiety disorder, of which FoF is only one aspect.

SPECIFIC PHOBIAS, A VERY COMMON DISORDER

The frequency of these particular forms of anxiety is very high in the general population, with a greater distribution in childhood and young/adult age, even if all age groups are affected.

But how widespread is the fear of flying?

According to recent surveys, in recent years in our country the percentage of people who have used air transport at least once has grown from 29 to 37%, with a prevalence of men over women (46% against 31%) [3], [4].

Of these people who have flown at least once, 33% admit to being afraid, and 10% declares that he will never fly again.

To obtain a global estimate, to these percentages it is necessary to add those relating to *regular fliers*": that is, those who travel regularly or very often.

This fact is not in itself a sign of tranquility regarding flying, given that many " *frequent fliers* " still experience discomfort or fear every time.

FoF in some way is around 50% of the population, similar data found in many countries.

In the United States, for example, a survey conducted by Pan American in 1975 found that approximately 16% of the US population was afraid of flying, and that 10% did not fly at all; five years later, another survey conducted this time by the Boeing Corporation reported that one in four American adults experienced fear or anxiety in the flight situation; finally in 2000 the percentage of Americans worried about flying was estimated at around 45%.

In Italy around 50% of people suffer from the fear of flying.

FOF AFFECTS BOTH SEXES

EVEN IF IN DIFFERENT WAYS

These disorders affect both sexes, although there is a slight prevalence of women compared to men (65% versus 48%), which seems to contrast with the fact that more men than women fly.

The interpretation of this data must also take into account other aspects, such as the different attitude of men and women towards the general idea of fear, strongly linked to cultural as well as personal elements.

Men, in fact, tend to deny the fear of flying, for which they do not ask for help; they therefore appear in the statistics only in extreme circumstances, while for women the request for intervention is generally simpler to formulate.

The tendency for men not to admit discomfort, in any form, is a fact well known to psychologists.

If we observe the quality of fear and the channels used to express it in both sexes, we note how in the female sample contents emerge that are more directly linked to a generalized psychological alarm, or to a generalized anxiety, linked to the fear of disaster and death (attack, hijacking , malfunction of the trolley or engines, accident); men, on the contrary, tend to express themselves more through somatic discomforts, discomforts that manifest themselves as fear of landing or take-off, as they are phases of flight in which pressure variations in the cockpit cause discomfort such as nausea, dizziness, headache.

Naturally, there is also fear of turbulence for the same reasons, fear of feeling ill in public and therefore shame, fear of feeling ill during the flight and of not being able to receive help.

Men and women are equal in the expression of claustrophobic / agoraphobic fears, such as the feeling of being trapped, of being at the mercy of someone you don't know and of not being able to get out when you want.

THE AGE OF ONSET IS VARIABLE

It is not possible to establish a precise age of onset of FoF , as it is very variable.

Some people remember having " *always* " been afraid of flying, while other people say that after an initial period of flights without problems they began to " *gradually* " become more and more afraid, still others report " *sudden* " onsets, sometimes although not always, following flight trauma.

Others, finally, trace the origin of the phenomenon precisely to advancing age, to the increase in awareness that this brings with it, to the increase in thoughts related to death.

The average age, between 40 and 50 years, seems to be the most affected, and in any case the one in which the majority of subjects decide, for different reasons but evidently relevant to this period of life, to concretely address the problem.

WHAT CAN TRIGGER FOF?

It can appear at any time in life, sometimes suddenly, more often gradually.

In some cases it is possible to trace, in the person's history, events to which the onset of the symptom can be traced back, or to which, if nothing else, the subject himself refers as the cause or event triggering the fear.

In the case of a sudden onset, there is often a " *traumatic* " event which is chosen as the sole and absolute triggering event.

In reality, as in any other case of more or less sudden onset of a phobic symptomatology, the cause can never be traced back to a single situation or event: more often we witness a complex chain of circumstances which, intertwining with the personality of the subject and his emotional experiences, evolve over time until they lead, often through a particular event that acts as a trigger, to the manifestation of discomfort.

These circumstances can be the most varied, and can have a particular meaning for the subject linked from time to time to his first experiences of interpersonal relationships, to his current most significant emotional relationships, to the internal dynamics of these relationships, including the personal sense attributed to the idea of bonding, separation and loss.

The set of these meanings can find, through different paths, a common container in the aerial object, which due to its peculiar characteristics of being a rapid instrument of distancing, separation and detachment, is well suited to collect the anxieties of death, extreme symbol of separation without return.

ARE WE ALL AFRAID OF FLYING?

There is a *"normal"* fear of the plane, which everyone feels, more or less consciously, and which can be considered as the signal of a particular activation (in English arousal) of our organism in view of a demanding task (= novelty, danger , etc.).

The external manifestation of such a fear is individual, and can oscillate between a total denial ("I'm not afraid at all") to the implementation of distracting techniques, such as reading, chatting with neighbors or crew members, sleeping , drinking alcohol, etc.

Certainly, the habit of flying has a very positive impact on this level of fear, as it reduces the *"novelty"* element.

However, it is not always sufficient, given that in some cases FoF appears in people who have already flown previously.

In any case, as long as it remains in these terms, this type of fear does not produce any avoidance reaction , and therefore does not limit or damage the life of the subject in a perceptible way, who manages to cope with this difficulty and respect his commitments without particular effort.

This fear can be considered "*healthy*" and therefore does not require any therapeutic intervention.

How do you determine when fear is no longer "*healthy*" but begins to border on pathology?

Of course it is not easy to establish a boundary between these two situations.

The only distinction is made up of the effects it produces on the life, activities and "freedom" of the individual.

We can say that FoF borders on pathology, on what we could call aerophobia, precisely when the level of fear is such as to cause intense anxiety reactions when taking the plane, or even before, at the mere thought of organizing the trip, or as the departure date approaches.

At this level of anxious reaction, an attempt at control may still be possible on the part of the subject, who will try to overcome the fear by devising various things, such as being accompanied by a trusted person, taking tranquilizers before and/or during the flight, asking on-board personnel to visit the cockpit.

Even if through these "*tricks*" the person manages to make the trip, it is evident that these same " *tricks* " end up negatively influencing the person's life and should still be considered for what they are: the signal of the need to resort to a consultation specialist.

But the element that fundamentally distinguishes and characterizes true FoF, so much so that we speak specifically of aerophobia in the strict sense, distinguishing this from " *simple* " fear and anxiety, is avoidance .

The person is so prey to the anguish due to flying and the very thought of flying, that he tends to avoid any situation that vaguely concerns him.

In this way, not only travel agencies and airports will be avoided (obviously), but also the very planning of business trips, holidays, etc.

If in the previous stage the subject's quality of life is already strongly compromised, given that everything involving air travel is experienced with anguish and attempts to overcome it end up causing considerable stress, when avoidance occurs, we witness a a dramatic narrowing of the margins of personal autonomy which, although often denied by the subject himself who perhaps claims to be able to do without it very well and in any case not to have any particular problem with the plane, in the long run tends to express itself in terms of discomfort, a sort of handicap.

With the appearance of avoidance and consequently with the restriction of the subject's autonomy, the repercussions begin, sometimes even serious ones, on his/her social and professional life.

At this point the aerophobia problem requires psychological treatment.

In this phase, the choice to face the problem and the ways in which it is faced are very linked to each person's personal life, and in particular to life events in relation to which a change is necessary for which the limitation becomes intolerable or strongly dangerous for the internal, emotional and/or professional balance of the subject. Regardless of gender, however, people who suffer from it experience very profound discomfort, both due to the intensity of the anxiety, which can reach the point of acute panic and which in any case makes them live in a situation of painful alarm throughout their day, and for the complete

upheaval of life that this condition causes.

In fact, to escape fears, people affected by these specific phobias take convoluted and complicated paths to avoid the object, place or situation that can trigger their fear.

It may happen that they often have to change jobs so as not to be forced to take an elevator, or the subway or, indeed, the plane.

For the same reasons their social relationships are heavily penalized; family relationships can suffer negative consequences due to the lack of autonomy of these subjects and the extreme dependence they develop on some of their family members who, in many cases, are involved in these fears as " *accompanists* ".

Phobic situations are endured with severe discomfort and fatigue and significantly interfere with normal daily routines.

More frequently, however, anxiety is generated not only by contact with the phobic stimulus but also by the mere thought of possible contact with this stimulus (anticipatory anxiety).

For this reason, feared situations and/or objects are avoided.

Avoidance reaction in turn generates a drastic limitation in the subject's personal, professional and relational life.

THE SYMPTOMS OF FOF

The most frequent symptoms of FoF are the somatic and the psychological ones individually or in association with each other.

Somatic symptoms affect the various systems:

-**cardiovascular** (tachycardia, peripheral vasoconstriction: cold sensation in the extremities, (chills);

-**respiratory** (tachypnea: short, superficial and frequent breathing, sensation of lack of air, sense of chest tightness);

-**glandular** (increased sweating);

-**gastrointestinal** (nausea, vomiting, feeling of abdominal swelling and heaviness, belching, abdominal cramps, sensation of " *butterflies in the stomach* ": diarrhea);

-**urogenital** (increased urge to urinate and diuresis);

-**muscular** (sense of tension and muscle pain, "*helmet headache*", stiffness and pain in the cervical region, abdominal cramps).

The psychological symptoms include a general feeling of painful anticipation, the fear of going mad or dying, the fear of losing control.

In FoF all these symptoms can present themselves, in different degrees of severity (from the acute crisis to a constant feeling of discomfort), both at the moment in which the subject finds himself in the stimulating situation (such as for example at the airport, at the time of check-in), when fastening your seat belt, just before the plane door is closed, during take-off, in flight when turbulence occurs), or even some time before the scheduled trip, in some cases even a month before, or to the sole evocation of thoughts or mental images regarding planes, flight, heights, travel.

Naturally, the symptoms present with individual differences.

The crisis manifests itself only when the subject comes into contact with the specific object of his fear, a fear linked to what the subject thinks may derive from that contact.

It is not necessary for the contact to be real, effective.

In some situations, just thinking or hearing about airplanes is enough to trigger a crisis of similar intensity to that aroused by concrete contact.

The fear of flying certainly has many causes partly

linked to subjective factors and experiences.

Overall, however, there are some elements more or less common to all those who suffer from FoF, just as there is a close affinity with the most well-known and widespread anxiety disorders, classified by Clinical Psychology.

If, in fact, we observe some of the criteria provided by the DSM V (Diagnostic and Statistic Manual, the diagnostic and statistical manual published by the American Psychiatric Association, which is generally referred to for the classification of psychological disorders) for Specific Phobia, we find the following symptoms:

A- Marked and persistent fear, excessive or unreasonable, caused by the presence or anticipation of a specific object or situation (e.g., flying, heights, animals, receiving an injection, seeing blood).

B- Exposure to the phobic stimulus almost invariably causes an immediate anxious response, which can take the form of a panic attack.

We specify that in children anxiety can be expressed by crying, with outbursts of anger, by tensing up, or by clinging to someone.

C- The person recognizes that the fear is excessive or unreasonable.

In children this feature may be absent.

D-The phobic situation is avoided or endured with intense anxiety or discomfort.

E- Avoidance , anticipatory anxiety, or discomfort in the feared situation significantly interferes with the person's normal routine, work (or school) functioning, or social activities or relationships, or distress is present marked for having the phobia.

Criterion A already includes, among the specific situations, flight.

In the vast majority of cases where FoF occurs, the airplane is perceived and feared as a particularly restricted, closed, overcrowded place, in which individual space is limited.

To this component which we could define as claustrophobic (always following the criteria of the DSM V) is added, however paradoxical it may appear from a strictly rational point of view, the sensation on the part of the subject of feeling projected into an empty space, completely open, in which no points of reference or boundaries are identified and which closely resembles agoraphobia.

We therefore always find ourselves in the context of disorders of the anxious sphere.

WHY BE AFRAID OF THE PLANE?

Let's say right away that this is not always true. It has already been said that, among the specific phobias, phobias for means of transport and aerophobia or FoF are considered separately .

In clinical reality, however, the simultaneous presence, in the same subject, of the fear of the plane and that of another means of transport, or even more than one, is frequently observed.

However, if we carefully observe the quality of the symptoms and the type of fear in both situations, we can note the presence of many similarities and areas of overlap, which leads us to suppose that we are faced with similar fears that from time to time they take on different forms.

For example, the fear of the ship shares with that of the plane both the fear of very vast or borderless spaces (such as the open sea and the sky), and the idea of being trapped and not being able to get off when you want.

The fear of cars has several similarities with aerophobia, such as the fear of speed, the feeling of being at the mercy of others and of having no control over the situation (fear of riding in a car with others), the fear of an accident, the fear of being trapped (fear of driving in traffic or tunnels) or of not being able to change direction when you want (fear of driving on the motorway), the fear of heights (fear of driving on viaducts or hairpin bends in mountain roads) .

Even when traveling by train, there is the fear of not having control over the vehicle and the feeling of being trapped.

This occurs more easily on modern trains, such as EuroStars, as they travel very long distances and have sealed windows.

There is a fear of speed and unpleasant physical sensations deriving from the oscillations of the train, of disasters, of the height of the viaducts and of the darkness of the tunnels.

Even the subway can trigger the claustrophobic fear of crowds and being underground.

When taking the bus, the main fear concerns crowding, the time between stops and traffic, all situations in which the person feels trapped and without the possibility of escape.

A common characteristic of all means of transport is that they remove, more or less quickly, those who use them.

This aspect which is, obviously, the institutional purpose of means of transport, for some people can take on the meaning of distancing and separation, with all that this entails for those who experience separation as a dangerous event in itself and, consequently, generating of strong anxiety.

Another common feature between the fear of flying and that of other means of transport is the fear of being unwell in a public situation, in which there is neither the possibility of fleeing at the first signs of unwellness (and therefore seeking shelter or hiding place), nor that of being able to be adequately helped, given that means of transport are not thought of as places where one can be helped promptly and effectively.

In some people, the feeling of shame is associated with the fear of losing self-control dramatically, in front of strangers imagined as indifferent or, worse, bad judgment.

WHY DOES THE PLANE CAUSE SO MANY FEARS?

Without a doubt, the fact that the plane leaves the

ground, remains suspended and moves in space, that is, it flies, is a very important component and a specificity of FoF .

In fact, man is not " *structurally* " prepared to do so, that is, he does not possess the right equipment, either in terms of genetic makeup or anatomical tools to fly.

Despite this, the evolution over time and the current state of the use of flight in different forms, as a means of transport (airliners), as a means of defense and war (military planes and helicopters), as a means of entertainment and exhilaration (paragliding, parachuting), as a means of space exploration (spaceships), makes us think about how man has always thought about flying with fear and, at the same time, with strong attraction and challenge, as indeed the myth of Icarus represents to indicate.

Given these premises, it must be recognized that the plane is a good container in which to bring together various types of anxieties and fears, so much so as to trigger an avoidance reaction .

This means that all you have to do is not take the plane and everything seems fine.

WHAT TO DO IN PRACTICE?

At this point the question arises spontaneously as to what can be done to overcome FoF.
Below we see some possible alternatives.

THE PHARMACOLOGICAL SOLUTION

It is no wonder that in a society like ours which tends to medicalize every aspect of life in order to increase the profits of pharmaceutical companies, even the first remedies that many specialists propose are pharmacological.
I also talk about them here as the first ones since I strongly advise against them, directing the reader towards other solutions, if only for the sometimes serious side effects of certain substances.
Evidently the drugs used in phobias (benzodiazepines, beta blockers, serotonin reuptake agents) do not represent a solution to FoF, also due to the side effects

that these drugs have.

It is important to keep in mind the dangerous synergy that can occur between these drugs and even the mild use of alcohol.

The effects of the simultaneous intake of benzodiazepines and alcohol can appear even when the ingestion of alcoholic beverages occurs 12 hours after the last administration of benzodiazepines.

However, if you opt for the pharmacological route, we strongly advise you to contact your doctor or, better yet, a psychiatrist, who will be able to better evaluate the response of the drug in relation to your individual need.

In fact, it will be important to know the individual reactivity to the drug, to avoid unpleasant side effects or paradoxes from occurring during the flight, such as an increase in the state of alarm which complicates the management of anxiety rather than helping the subject to reduce it, or that the sedative effect manifests itself, not during the flight, but subsequently, once disembarked and when there is no longer the need, often leaving the person in a state of stupor just when he should be at his best.

IN-FLIGHT MEDICAL ASSISTANCE

The problem of medical assistance during flights is

particularly acute today and the major airlines are taking steps to modernize on-board medical equipment. For example, before long, we will find telemedicine equipment on airplanes for the diagnosis of cardiac disorders.

While the problem of who is authorized to intervene competently in the particular situation of an air journey remains debated, since not even long-haul flights require the presence of a doctor, the medical equipment on board provides, again depending on the duration of the journey, a first aid kit which also contains anxiolytics, which can be used by the flight staff, and a doctor's kit, containing a wide range of medicines, which only the doctor can use after authorization from the commander.

Therefore, in case of acute or intense anxiety, the on-board staff can be notified and, if necessary, they will administer the anxiolytic.

There is no doubt that in this case the ability and sensitivity of the cabin crew are important.

BEHAVIORAL THERAPY

Behavioral therapy arises from the learning theories of Pavlov and Skinner .

According to these theories, certain behaviors and emotions such as the fear of flying originate from incorrect learning which makes it impossible for the subject to distinguish between truly dangerous stimuli and harmless ones.

The subject, in fact, produces a conditioned response of fear even if he finds himself in the presence of stimuli which, due to their characteristics, should be considered neutral or even pleasant and therefore to be sought and not avoided.

Consequently, the therapy is based on the idea of opposing counter-conditioning to the conditioning that is at the basis of the development of the phobia.

This can happen, for example, by exposing the subject to anxiety-provoking situations until this passes.

One type of treatment is **Systematic Desensitization.**

After inducing a deep state of relaxation in the person presenting the phobia, in our case the fear of flying, through the techniques illustrated below, he is made to imagine a progressively more and more frightening series and scenes, obviously in our case related to flying.

BIOFEEDBACK.
WHAT IT IS FOR

Biofeedback, which literally means biological back information, refers to a particular category of electronic instruments and devices which allow, thanks to special sensors connected to the person, to place under voluntary control those bodily functions which are normally found outside of awareness. and of the will.

Thanks to this equipment, the psychologist expert in bio-feedback can guide the subject suffering from FoF to modify their dysfunctional cognitive, motor and neurovegetative responses, allowing the establishment of more appropriate habits and reactions.

Biofeedback is an electronic device that allows the control of involuntary reactions through the detection and evaluation of appropriate physiological indices.

Emotions are obviously also included among these involuntary reactions and the interest in biofeedback procedures consists above all in making emotions manifest.

Some will wonder how some parameters of the physical and vegetative state (heart rate, peripheral temperature, muscle tension, skin electrical potential) can be the index of our emotional situation and how is it possible that by managing to control these parameters we are able to modify, correct and improve our emotional responses.

To understand the relationship between an emotion, such as anxiety, and its physical manifestations, it is necessary to know the nature and origin of the emotion. The initial assumption is that emotion includes two aspects: the bodily response that characterizes it and the awareness we have of it.

PRIMARY AND SECONDARY EMOTIONS

Primary emotions, as Charles Darwin first demonstrated, are innate and depend on instinctive responses.

The interesting fact is that fundamental emotions, such as anger, fear, joy, etc., have proven, after extensive studies, to be universal, that is, present in all human populations and in all cultures.

Relevant is the fact that even the typical facial expressions of these emotions are universal. Thus an

Australian aborigine will immediately be able to tell what emotion it is, simply by looking at the photo of an European and vice versa.

This is made possible by the fact that there are precise areas of the central nervous system where the expression and interpretation of these emotions are, so to speak, " *coded* ".

Secondary emotions, on the other hand, are acquired and depend on the associative relationships that are established, based on lived experiences, between certain situations and particular emotional responses.

From a physical point of view, primary and secondary emotions have effector pathways in common, given that they use the same nervous circuits and manifest themselves in the same way at a bodily level, despite having " *seat* " in different districts of the Central Nervous System.

This very simply means that the resulting physical correlates, i.e. the external expression, are similar.

What changes, in addition to the cognitive connotation of the emotion, are the processes that generate them.

The common pathway is activated after certain stimuli are recognized as associated with a particular emotional response on the basis of instinctive predispositions (primary emotions) or experience (secondary emotions).

FoF, as is easy to imagine, is a particular type of anxiety and therefore a secondary emotion in which, as happens with other emotions, the presence of three components is recognised:

A- the stimulus

B- the answer

C- the internal process which, activated by the stimulus, leads to the manifestation of anxiety.

The central factor in the genesis of FoF and therefore of a particular type of anxiety that manifests itself in a very precise and specific context, is the internal process.

RELAXATION TECHNIQUES IN PRACTICE

The best and most effective solution to overcome FoF is the adoption of relaxation techniques that allow us to approach the moment of flight and undertake it with peace of mind.

However, the two things are not separated from each other.

Anxiety, in fact, tends to " *cumulate* " as the critical moment approaches.

The adoption of these techniques, at least in the period before the actual flight, meaning the period before both the previous days and the hours that we still have to spend at the airport for check-in, will be able to significantly reduce anticipatory anxiety, allowing us to play down the event.

There are many relaxation techniques and everyone will be able to choose the ones they deem most suitable for themselves.

Some are of Western origin and others that refer to Eastern traditions such as Yoga or Qi-gong .

They are all equally valid, even if we will limit ourselves to describing exercises coming mainly from techniques of Western origin, with one exception, due to their greater applicability in a particular situation such as that of an airplane, which certainly does not allow the practice of exercises for example Yoga.

I preferred to expand the possibilities so that everyone can find the one best suited to themselves.

However, we consider the knowledge and constant practice of oriental techniques to be very useful, precisely because the habit of relaxation, however obtained, induces greater ease in obtaining the relaxation itself even with different methods.

Whatever the technique adopted and whatever the exercises performed, it is absolutely necessary to remember that it is important to practice the exercises in the period preceding the moment in which it will be necessary to use them.

Some of these techniques require a certain period of training to deepen the ability to induce the desired relaxation.

It would therefore be good practice for these techniques

to be performed methodically and regularly, regardless of the need to fly.

However, they will be useful in reducing our level of anxiety and stress even in everyday life.

In fact, we must not think that stress is just a figure of speech or a fashionable word.

It is widely documented in the scientific field how the constant adoption of relaxation techniques allows us to significantly reduce (and easily measurable with a simple blood test) cortisol , a hormone produced in excess by our body when we are under stress.

However, if our practice has not been constant, it is useful to remember to " *refresh* " it at least a week before having to take the plane, at this point on a daily basis.

Whatever technique is adopted, it is absolutely necessary to remember that it is important to practice the exercises in the period preceding the moment in which it will be necessary to use them.

Before moving on to illustrate the various relaxation techniques, we indicate a couple of preparatory exercises that are extremely useful for preparing for the subsequent exercises.

LEARN TO RELAX THE BODY, WELCOMING IT

(20-25 Minutes, 2 times a day)

This is an important exercise that can be considered both an introduction to actual relaxation techniques and a powerful exercise in its own right.

Precisely for this reason, some easy manual techniques have been described, derived from Shiatsu but practicable by anyone, which make it possible to facilitate the dissolution of some emotional tensions which, as always happens, take the form of muscular stiffness in some parts of the body.

Before starting, read slowly and imagine how the exercise we propose is carried out.

If necessary, read it two or three times aloud to make it clear to you.

Under no circumstances should you consult the text while doing it at the risk of interrupting your relaxation.

Try the manual techniques indicated several times to become familiar with the muscular-emotional tensions that arise in some parts of our body.

RELAX YOUR BODY

If you are at home, lie down comfortably, or sit in the armchair, like the one on the plane, perhaps reclining it slightly backwards.

If you are taking off and have to keep the seat not reclined, the exercise can still be performed.

Close your eyes to no longer be hindered by visual stimuli.

Certainly the auditory ones, i.e. the noises coming from other passengers, from the stewardesses and in any case from the plane, will continue to arrive.

That's okay, welcome them without rejecting them as sometimes happens when welcoming the deafening noise of a storm or the noise of traffic.

Once this is done, begin to evaluate the body's support points: the head on the pillow or headrest, at the level of the nape of the neck, the shoulders, the back, the arms on the bed or on the armrests of the airplane seat, as well as the shoulders, elbows and hands.

In the lower part, the pelvis is supported on the buttocks while the legs, which continue into the calves and feet, are in turn supported by the heels.

Let yourself go according to your weight, adapting as

best as possible to the shape of your airplane seat, perhaps with the help of a small pillow or blanket which is never missing on airplanes, and evaluate the changes brought about by this simple relaxation position.

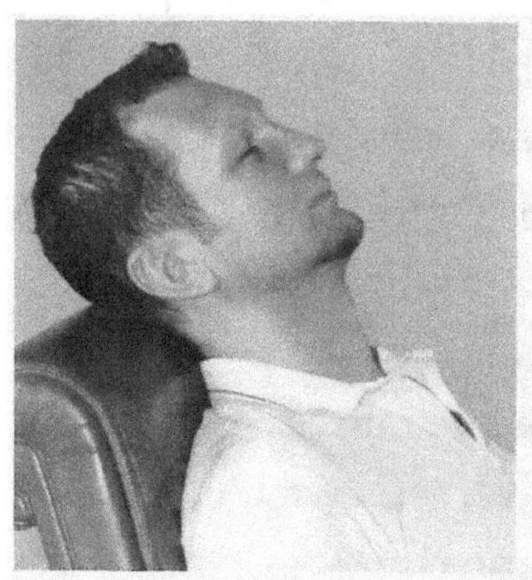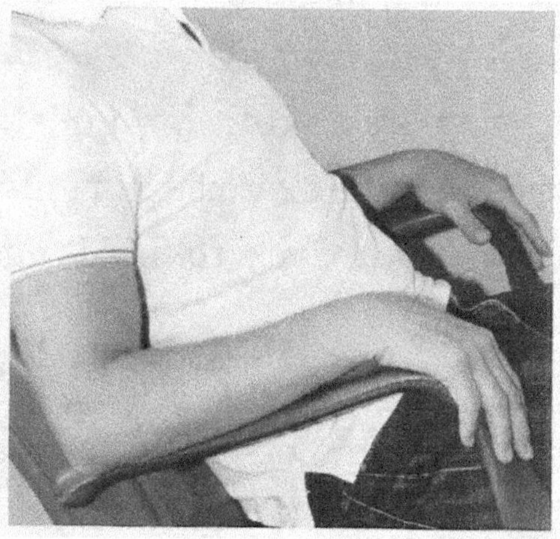

Also become aware of the contact of your clothes on your body.

This perception will allow you to improve concentration.

Please discover this contact with pleasure.

It goes without saying that it is absolutely essential that clothes are loose, comfortable and not tight.

Completely relax your face, which often looks more like a generally tense mask, whose frowning forehead you can loosen.

Feel the wrinkles and folds disappear, to feel the scalp

and temples, as well as the eyebrows and bridge of the nose, relax.

If you can, try to move slowly, contracting and relaxing the skin of the head, i.e. the area on which the hair is implanted, and also the ears.

By paying attention to these details, you are immersed in listening to your body.

Now let's get to the eyelids. Do they flap imperceptibly? It doesn't matter, just let it go, it's natural.

Concentrate your attention for a while on your cheeks, probably contracted because your jaws are clenched.

BECOME AWARE OF IT,
RELAX YOUR MOUTH

Gently touch the jaw with your fingers, preferably the thumb, especially where it articulates with the temporal bone.

Is it stiff because the masticatory muscles are contracted?

It is possible, given that anxiety-provoking situations tend to make these muscles contract unconsciously.

By pressing these muscles delicately but firmly, starting approximately from the side of the ear - it is best to proceed simultaneously on both sides - while still pressing, slide the thumb following the jaw up to the chin.

The maneuver is repeated until the muscles begin to loosen.

Is the mouth ajar? Perfectly.

Abandon any attitude, any mask.

Evaluate carefully the changes brought about by this relaxation of the skin and muscles.

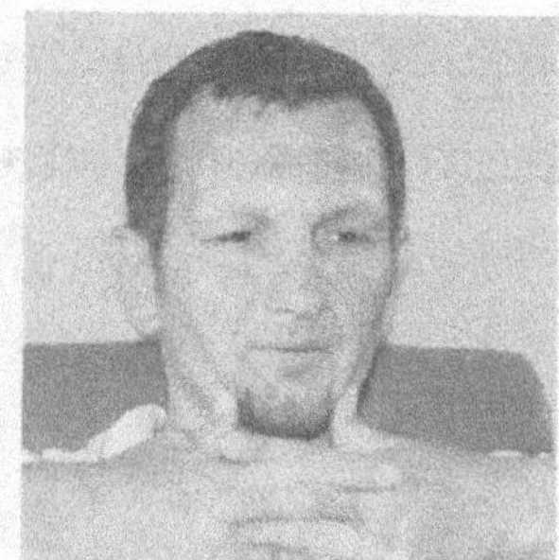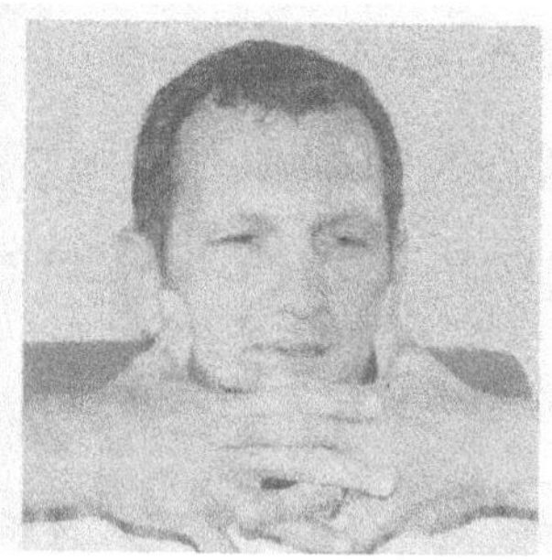

Then, let your head rest on the cushion or headrest of the seat, calculate the surface area of the back of your neck that rests on it.

Let go of your shoulders too, another point of tension, let them fall, relax your back.

The neck, which is located in the middle, relaxes.

If you don't succeed on the first shot, press lightly with the index and middle fingers of the hand on the opposite side on the area between the neck and the shoulder joint.

You will likely find an area that is tense, perhaps stiff and painful to pressure.

Without exaggerating, press with two fingers until you feel a little pain, not too much.

Remain still on the point with that pressure until the pain subsides and then disappears.

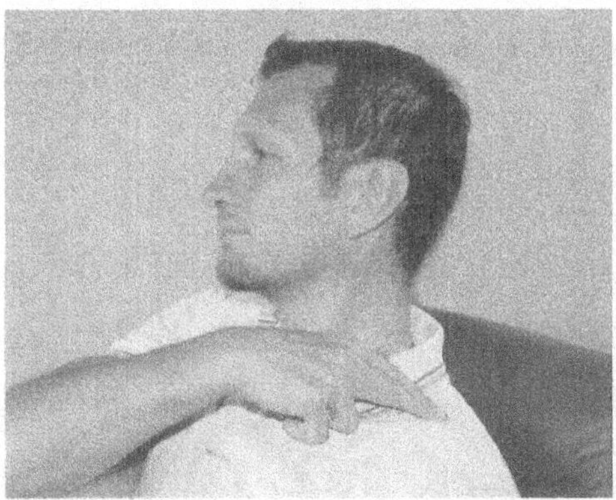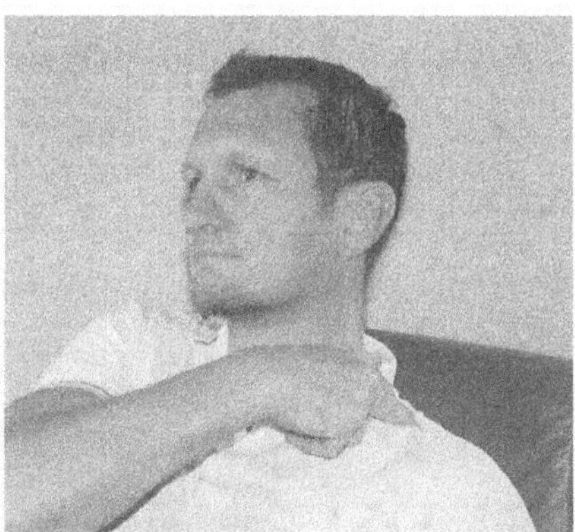

If you want, at that point you can repeat the maneuver, increasing the pressure.

Eventually you will notice that your neck has relaxed and contracted.

It will even seem like it has grown longer.

Evaluate as best you can the responses that come to you from this part of the body.

Get to know each other.

Is your neck stiff and you can't keep it relaxed on the headrest of your airplane seat?

Run your fingers behind your neck, sideways to your ear.

With some attention you will be able to identify small rounded emergencies on both sides.

These too will appear more or less painful when pressed. With your thumb, press them lightly until the pain goes away.

Then relax your back, imagining and feeling it.

Let it go as if it could expand; relax the shoulder blades, the entire spine, even the lumbar part, the kidneys, generally arched, tense.

By letting go of your back, at the same time relax your chest, and you will be able to realize that your breathing is gradually freeing itself from muscular constraints.

If your breathing remains labored, run your thumb along the center line of your body from the throat, running over the sternum, the central bone of the rib cage.

Scrolling with your finger you will notice that the bone changes inclination at a certain point, forming a slightly raised angle.

Try pressing delicately and possibly with greater force on this corner and a little below, about three fingers, on another point that appears painful. Maintain light pressure until the pain goes away.

It seems that the air enters and exits more easily, little by little.

If you now release the abdominal muscles, the belly, and in particular the abdominal band, you can feel more complete breathing, i.e. both thoracic and abdominal.

The belly and chest breathe at the same rhythm.

If this is not the case, form a sort of wedge with the fingers of your hand and go to the solar plexus, just below where the sternum ends.

With this wedge formed by your fingers, press with some force for half a minute, then let go.

Your diaphragm will move more freely and your breathing will be deeper.

Now focus your attention on your arms, locate them well in the space, evaluate their support points and contact with clothing.

Let your arms, elbows, forearms and hands fall dead weight.

Try to determine what the heaviness in the arms is: it is a sign of lowering muscle tone.

The arms have a certain weight: try to calculate it.

This lowering of muscle tone involves a decompression of the muscles on the vessels, thus allowing better blood circulation which often expresses itself with a pleasant warming or with slight itching, particularly felt on the back of the hands, or with pulsations on the fingertips, under the nails.

Paying attention, focusing on the body, will allow you to eliminate all thoughts.

YOU ARE LISTENING TO YOUR BODY. IT ONLY MATTER WHAT YOU DO, MUSCLE RELAXATION, AND WHAT YOU FEEL

While the arms continue to relax and regenerate, also relax the pelvis: the buttocks, the belly and the lower abdomen, the muscles of the perineum.

Do you feel tension in this area? It's time to do a few exercises that allow you to relax the lower part of the pelvis.

Contract your pelvic floor muscles forcefully and after 10 seconds release them.

Rest for a moment and repeat the exercise about ten times.

What does this mean in practice? Think about what type of muscle contraction you would use if you wanted to block yourself when you pee.

It involves activating, contracting, the same muscles.

Continue by stretching your legs in the same way, that is, fixing your attention on them, trying to see them mentally and abandoning them to their weight, a bit as if you were disconnecting them, resting your thighs, knees and legs on your calves, feet on heels.

Try to evaluate the weight, the heaviness, the earth's attraction and also this gentle, progressive heat, which is particularly felt at knee height.

RELAX YOUR SPIRIT

As your body relaxes in this way, you can allow your nervous system and mind to stabilize as well.

To do this, just allow yourself to fall into a different level of consciousness, between waking and sleeping.

Then imagine falling asleep in the way you know well.

Therefore, take the image of drowsiness and allow yourself to be calmly lowered into an area that may initially seem darker, due to the converging of the eyeballs downwards, as if you were looking inside the nose.

In particular, you can evaluate this impression of descent every time you exhale the air. You can even use this exhalation to accompany this descent, in successive degrees, each time a little more deeply, into an area that is certainly darker, but also and above all calmer.

Little by little external noises no longer disturb you, on the contrary they can serve as a point of reference, they can allow you to appreciate the quiet that is established internally compared to the noises and agitation that are outside.

Every time you exhale the air, you let your mind sink a little deeper, to the very edges of sleep.

At this point the time has come to include a further step in this exercise, that is, visualize a color, your favorite, and see it flow inside you, in a kind of circuit.

With the help of thought, when we inhale, we imagine a beam of colored light (generally relaxing colors such as green or blue are chosen) and we see it flowing downwards, starting from the mouth, up to the area placed below the navel.

From here the colored light continues, then goes up the back and, past the head, reaches the mouth where it is emitted at the moment of exhalation.

You thus enter into closer, more intimate communication with the body, which is there, motionless.

Welcome all the new perceptions that emanate from it, appreciate this relaxation, this balance that is established between the body and the mind.

It is body-spirit harmony.

Remain like this for a few moments, listening to yourself... Silence...

Every time you put this method into practice, which is actually very simple and natural, you will not only allow your body to recover, but you will also re-establish your entire nervous system and, above all, you will set your ability to control and lucidity in motion.

You will increase your potential, your personality.

AND NOW GET BACK

Once the training, or in any case the execution of the exercise, is finished, do not immediately go back to work.

Above all, never forget to recover to restore your activity tone.

Therefore, always start by breathing, once or twice, allowing yourself to rise to the surface.

Recover, by shaking slightly, the feet, hands and face, which are three cardinal points of the body.

Then stretch your legs, even the space under the seat is enough, stretch your back and arms forward and don't hesitate to stretch, as if you had spent a wonderful night.

Don't open your eyes until you are sure that you have completely recovered your tone and energy.

To carry out this simple and natural exercise, ten minutes are enough, a short period of time that you will easily find twice a day or which, in any case, can always be performed when needed, also as an introductory technique to the exercises explained later.

WHAT ARE THE ADVANTAGES

OF THIS EXERCISE?

Firstly, a more precise knowledge of yourself. " *Know thyself* " takes shape.

Then, muscle relaxation will bring you an unparalleled state of physical well-being.

You will feel perfectly comfortable in your skin.

The recovery of energy following these minutes of relaxation can be compared to two and a half hours of sleep.

Finally, this mental relaxation, in addition to making you discover an unsuspected mastery and developing your potential, will little by little serve as an incentive, in the sense that throughout the day you will progressively want to rediscover this state of inner calm, serenity, lucidity. .

In this way, little by little, you will become aware of the bodily tensions that will inevitably arise during the day, in order to be able to loosen them quickly, easily, anywhere and at any time, thus determining mental deactivation and

psychic harmony.

This is the indispensable premise for deactivating the psychological mechanism that leads to FoF .

As regards the subsequent, more specific and targeted exercises, the practice of this preparatory exercise, in addition to progressively reducing your state of anxiety, will greatly facilitate the achievement of the best state of relaxation for the practice of Autogenic Training and Progressive Relaxation according to Jacobson .

DO YOU REALLY KNOW HOW TO RELAX? DO THE FIST TEST

At this point we could open a parenthesis for those of you who have difficulty experiencing what exactly relaxation and muscle relaxation is.

Some, in fact, performing the previous exercise, will have wondered whether they were really able to perform it correctly and achieve true relaxation.

In this case we advise you to perform a small, very easy exercise: close your eyes, extend one arm forward horizontally, make a very strong fist, feel the tension in the hand, wrist and forearm.

Now raise your closed fist and notice the increase in this tension in your forearm.

Then let your arm fall, opening your fist.

Notice the perceptions gathered after the tension.

Also compare with the other arm.

Let yourself go completely. This is what muscle relaxation is.

Thanks to concentration, you will be able to evaluate these perceptions without having to amplify them through tension.

The only difference lies in the point from which you start: in this case you start from a hypertensive muscle tone and therefore it is easy to perceive its lowering of tension.

In the previous method, you started from a normal posture tone and tried to lower it towards the basic tone. The difference is smaller, therefore more difficult to perceive.

Train, and little by little, by perfecting your concentration, you will come to perceive these subtle changes.

Another exercise that can easily make us perceive the difference between relaxation and rigidity is that of compressions of the phalanges of the feet.

Standing, with your feet apart and approximately shoulder-width apart, keeping your knees slightly bent, place one foot on the toe resting on a carpet and gently compress your toes towards the plantar side.

It may be slightly painful at first, although with practice

the stiffness of the back of the foot will tend to decrease. After a few seconds, kick backwards and place your foot on the floor.

Compare the state of the foot that "worked" with the other and you will notice the difference. Naturally we then proceed with the other foot.

AUTOGENIC TRAINING. WHAT IS THAT

Autogenic Training (AT) is a Western relaxation technique created by the doctor H. Schultz between the 1920s and 1930s and developed by him starting from studies on hypnosis.

Unlike the latter, which requires external directives, AT makes the person less tied to dependence on the therapist, to become himself the author of his own change and well-being.

In fact, the term Autogenic highlights how psychic and somatic changes are caused independently by the practitioner, adapting the method to his or her own needs.

WHAT IT IS FOR

In general, the practice of Autogenic Training influences various functions dependent on the Vegetative Nervous System such as breathing, blood circulation and metabolism.

These are in fact the main physiological functions that are activated by FoF .

It also allows you to change your mood and in particular attenuates emotional states and anxiety, leading to an ever greater degree of relaxation, well-being and psychosomatic balance.

In fact, it allows you to combat stress, muscular and mental tension, lack of energy, anxiety and its organic somatizations:

tremors, insomnia, sweating, tachycardia, chest tightness, gastritis, colitis, constipation, bronchial asthma, nervous tics.

HOW IT DOES

The principle on which autogenic training is based is calm, a state that is achieved progressively and gradually through a series of standard exercises which, by modifying the body state (acting on muscles, blood vessels, heart, breathing, abdominal organs and head), cause changes on a psychological level.

Below we illustrate some exercises that can easily be practiced both on the plane and in the hours before the flight, remembering that to optimize the results it is still important to practice the exercises with a certain consistency and not just implement them at the moment of need.

THE BASIC POSITIONS

AT exercises can be performed in all positions, although usually more relaxing positions are chosen, such as sitting and lying down.

Here we will illustrate the exercises only in a sitting position, which is practically the only one that can be adopted on an airplane.

The sitting position 1;

Position 1, also called the **box coachman's position**, is the original one adopted by H. Schultz .

He had copied it by observing the coachmen of Viennese carriages resting between one customer and another.

To take it on, a simple stool is sufficient.

To achieve the necessary somatic adjustment, it is not necessary to excessively flex the trunk forward; this would result in compression on the abdomen and the need to lean on the arms.

The legs must be slightly apart at an angle of approximately 75-80 degrees; the forearms, passively abandoned on the thighs, will rest on them more or less between the proximal third and the middle third of the distance between the elbow and the tips of the extended fingers.

In the coachman's position, the attitude of the head is determined by the subject's structure and his postural habits.

In brachytypes, that is, in stockier people, the head can easily hang forward, while on the contrary, people with long necks tend more easily to let their heads fall backwards.

The flexed head position is the position generally assumed.

The position of the box coachman allows a limited support surface for the forearms, more or less corresponding to the proximal part of the middle portion of the forearm itself; for this reason the hands hang freely in the void.

This position is not suitable for obese people, pregnant women and those suffering from breathing and cervical vertebrae disorders.

To these people we directly recommend sitting position 2, also described by Shultz and in any case a valid alternative to the other, in an airplane seat.

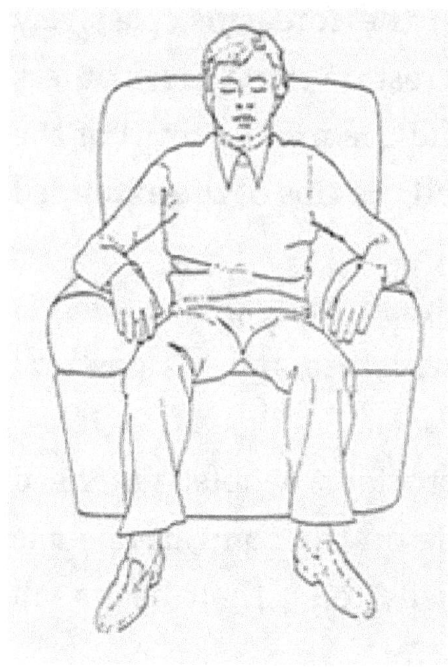

Sitting position 2

To implement it, says Schultz , the back must be able to comfortably adhere to the backrest and the legs must not be pushed forward.

The armrests of the chair must be positioned so that the arms rest on them passively and without muscular tension; the forearm must form an obtuse angle of approximately 120-130 degrees with the arm, while the legs must not be crossed, the hands must not touch each other (just as they must not touch each other in the coachman's position).

It should be noted that in the sitting position, Schultz sees an analogy with those postures which in the Indian tradition are the most suitable for allowing easy meditation.

BEFORE STARTING THE REAL EXERCISES

It is important that clothing is comfortable and not restrictive, it is a good idea to loosen belts, ties, remove watches, glasses and shoes.

In order to verify the validity of the exercises carried out, it is useful to get into the habit of carrying with you, when traveling by plane, a small notepad and a pen with which to briefly record the date, time and place where you find yourself and your position (corridor side, window side), the dominant thoughts and the physical sensations felt, looking for to quantify them (for example: normal heartbeat, slow, fast, very fast, etc.) The same type of recording will be done at the end of the exercises.

In addition to being useful to you, to verify how FoF evolves over time and the practice of the exercises, these notes could also be useful to any psychologist who follows you to obtain the cognitive-behavioral changes necessary to obtain more lasting results.

HOW THE EXERCISES ARE PERFORMED

After assuming sitting position 1 or 2, close your eyes and deepen the breathing that we normally do.

After a while, try to do a 4-stage breathing as per the following scheme:

Inhalation (deep but not excessive, that is, it does not put too much tension on the rib cage)

Break

Deep exhalation but done very slowly.

It is good that the exhalation lasts slightly longer than the inhalation and is as complete as possible.

It is essential, at least for the first time, to get into the habit of "*counting*" your breath.

In practice this means, for example, inhaling to a slow count of 1 to 6 (or more), then taking the first pause to a count of 4.

Exhale for a count of 8 (or more) at the same speed and then pause for a second count of 2.

Don't worry, after a while this breathing pattern will become you automatic.

DO DEEP BREATHING

Correct breathing must be both thoracic and diaphragmatic.

We will try to explain what these two terms mean, so that everyone can verify the correctness of what they are doing.

When we inhale, our lungs must expand, thus causing the individual pulmonary alveoli to expand to accommodate more *"clean"* air, i.e. rich in oxygen, while when we exhale the opposite happens and the air rich in carbon dioxide is emitted outside.

For this to happen, it is necessary for the rib cage, thanks to its structure, to expand and contract alternately.

In reality, during inhalation the rib cage, thanks to the action of the intercostal muscles, dilates slightly and rises.

If our breathing, however, is limited to this mechanism, it will always be very short and

superficial and if our need for air becomes greater, it will quickly become fast and labored.

For our breathing to be deep it is important that another muscle comes into action, the diaphragm, a muscle that separates the chest from the abdomen with its dome shape.

Often anxious people are unable to use the diaphragm correctly and so their breathing will always and only be thoracic, often ending up in a situation of shortness of breath, which in turn can induce feelings of fear in people, thus starting a cycle vicious in which fear makes breathing labored but the perception of one's own labored breathing stimulates an increase in fear.

One of the purposes of practicing the relaxation exercises that are illustrated in this text is precisely to induce deep breathing, both thoracic and diaphragmatic.

We can test the difference between these two breaths by lying down on a mat or carpet and starting to breathe automatically, as we usually do.

Let's now place a hand on the abdomen, below the navel. If the hand rises rhythmically as the lower part of the abdomen inflates and deflates, this is a sign that our breathing is deep enough and effective, therefore also diaphragmatic, otherwise our breathing will be exclusively or predominantly thoracic and therefore insufficient.

In this position we will try to deepen our breathing until we begin to perceive the movement of our hand.

In order to improve and make breathing more effective, it can be helpful to press the abdomen while also gently squeezing the rib cage with the other hand.

This will allow us to make the exhalation deeper, also making us understand how far this can go, and above all making the inhalation deeper too.

During breathing, thoughts of all types may arrive.

Don't worry about chasing them away but, rather, let them come in.

Simply limit yourself to concentrating on breathing and the correct duration of the 4 stages, " *counting the breath*

".

Don't worry about chasing away thoughts at any cost, rather let them enter yours head.

Simply concentrate on the 4 stages of breathing: inhalation; break; exhalation; break.

AUTOGENIC TRAINING

HEAVINESS EXERCISE

(About 10 min).

The sequence involves the progressive, slow analysis of the various parts of the body starting with the right arm, then moving on to the left arm, right leg, left leg, abdomen, chest, shoulders and back, repeating the formula:

" *I am calm..., calm..., perfectly calm... My right arm is heavy..., heavy..., very heavy... I feel completely relaxed ...*"

Then we move on to the left arm:

" *I am calm..., calm..., perfectly calm... My left arm is heavy..., heavy..., very heavy... I feel completely relaxed... *"

At this point we move on to the right leg:

" *I am calm..., calm..., perfectly calm... My right leg is heavy..., heavy..., very heavy... I feel completely relaxed ...*"

Repeat the formula 5-6 times.

With the same formula we then proceed in sequence on the other parts of the body.

While repeating the formulas, concentrate on the limb that is relaxing, forming a mental image of it and visualizing the muscles that progressively relax.

Especially in the initial sessions, which are essential to achieve a good ability to induce relaxation, it is advisable to linger on each limb 5-6 times or more, continuously before moving on to the other limb.

HEAT EXERCISE

(About 10 min.)

The sequence is the same as the previous exercise and therefore also in this case it is important to start with the right arm, then move on to the left arm, right leg, left leg, abdomen, chest, shoulders and back.

Even the formula is the same, replacing " *heavy* " with the word " *hot* ":

" *I am calm..., calm... perfectly calm... My right arm is warm..., warm... very warm... and I feel completely relaxed ...*"

We then move on to the left arm:

" *I am calm..., calm..., perfectly calm... My left arm is warm..., warm..., very warm... I feel completely relaxed ...*"
Repeat the formula 5-6 times.

Especially at the beginning it may be necessary to repeat the formula a few more times, it doesn't matter.

It is necessary to continue until the sensation of heat appears.

The same formula was then followed for the other parts of the body.

While repeating the formulas, concentrate on the limb that is being warmed up, visualizing the muscles that progressively relax and the capillaries that are supplied and dilated by the blood flow.

You see the bright red blood flowing from the larger arteries all the way down to the smaller ones, up to the capillaries.

By flowing in this way, the blood progressively tends to warm up until it reaches a pleasant level of warmth that envelops us.

Especially in the initial sessions, it is advisable to focus on each limb 5-6 times continuously before moving on to the other limb.

HEART EXERCISE

(About 10 min.)

Concentrate on the heart, visualize it in the center of the chest, repeating the formula:

" *I am calm..., calm..., perfectly calm... My heart is strong and beats calmly... calm and regular... I feel calm and calm ...*"

Visualize the heart beating slowly and calmly, with a powerful and tranquil calm.

Repeat the formula 5-6 times or as many times as necessary to obtain the desired effect.

According to Schultz, in well-trained individuals, the heart rate can be deliberately accelerated

or slowed down with the appropriate formulas.

This is even more true if you combine the various exercises, and this one in particular, with the 4-stage breathing exercises as explained above.

It is important to respect the timing of breathing in 4 stages given that this rhythm breathing alone, acting on the Autonomic Nervous System, is able to slow down the heartbeat.

In reality this technique was already well known, in *"prescientific"* times, to Yoga practitioners.

BREATHING EXERCISE

(About 10 min.)

Visualizing the body, and in particular the lungs, concentrate on the breathing, repeating the formula:

" I am calm..., calm... perfectly calm...My breathing is calm and regular... I feel calm and calm ..."

Until we reach:

" My breathing becomes deeper and deeper... calm...,

regular... I feel calm and peaceful... I am deeply relaxed ..."
Start by seeing the air entering from the mouth, going down the throat until it reaches the two lungs, right and left, and then, progressively, move the visualization to the center of the body, seeing the chest and abdomen expanding, the shoulders that widen as you move upwards, and finally imagining the whole body as a large lung:

"*my body breathes with me... My breath breathes me...*"
Repeat the formula 5-6 times.

Help can come from imagining yourself immersed in the sea in the form of a sponge that inflates and deflates to the rhythm of the waves that follow one another large and slow above and below the sea. Imagine that breathing takes on the rhythm of the sponge and that our entire body contracts and relaxes following this rhythm.

In fact, the respiratory rhythm, with its alternation of expansion and contraction, is the most obvious rhythm of the human body and is easy to follow.

SOLAR PLEXUS EXERCISE

(About 10 min.)
Concentrate on the central area between the sternum and the navel and repeat the formula:

" I am calm..., calm... perfectly calm... My solar plexus is hot..., very hot... My solar plexus is hot and radiating heat... I feel calm and calm ... I am deeply relaxed ..."

Repeat the formula 5-6 times.

Imagine a small sun placed in the abdomen that spreads heat all around or the blood that flows into that area bringing vital energy and warmth, heat that dissolves all tensions.

You can place a hand on this point, feeling your breathing rhythm and feeling your hand warmed by this sun.

FOREHEAD EXERCISE

(About 10 min.)

Concentrate on the forehead, initially trying to perceive the tensions that are often concentrated precisely on the forehead, trying to loosen them.

Start repeating the formula:

" I am calm... calm..., perfectly calm... My forehead is cool... pleasantly cool..... I feel calm and peaceful... I feel completely relaxed ..."

Repeat the formula 5-6 times.

An effective image could be to see yourself lying on a lawn or on a beach, with the sun warming your body while a pleasant breeze touches your forehead.

RECOVERY EXERCISES

(About 5-6 min.)

TA session , perform small movements called recovery exercises. They consist of flexion and extension movements of the feet and hands until the arms and legs are involved, initially small and gradually more and more energetic.

Then breathe deeply and open your eyes.

THE FORMULAS AND PROPOSALS

Together with the "standard" formulas, personal formulas can be inserted aimed at resolving any recurring disturbing situations, which continually arise from deep within and which often originate from an anxious complex such as the fear of the dark, of certain animals, of speaking in public, to deal with a certain situation.

In our case, obviously, we will deal with FoF.

After visualizing the disturbing situation, insert a short formula that tends to emotionally bring it back to normality.

For example, we could think: when I'm inside a plane I feel calm and relaxed.

Or again: when I take a plane trip I am calm and happy to

fly.

PROGRESSIVE RELAXATION ACCORDING TO JACOBSON

Starting from the assumption that emotions arise from thought and, consequently, even if in an absolutely unconscious manner, some muscles that depend on the emotion itself are activated, Edmund Jacobson, around the 1930s, Jacobson developed a very simple and effective method which, by acting on the muscles, i.e. starting from the effect of emotions on the body, aimed to bring the mind back to a state of calm.

This relaxation technique is useful for lowering tension, promoting sleep and general mental and physical relaxation.

The goal is to regain contact with the body and deepen knowledge.

This is achieved analytically by acting on the various segments and regions with alternating muscle tension and relaxation.

Tensing a muscle to the maximum and immediately relaxing it makes you aware of tensions that you are normally not aware of.

According to E. Jacobson, any tension in the various regions of the body is connected to different states of mind:

-the **fear** of not controlling situations and the inability to make decisions;

-the **chest** to the fear of expressing emotional emotions, love;

-the **pelvis** to the fear of expressing one's sexuality;

-the **lower limbs** to the fear of static, waiting, silence.

The exercises are performed in the same positions as Autogenic Training after taking a few deep breaths.

Here we will only take into consideration the two sitting positions because they are more suitable for the airplane and indicated for those who feel the need to promptly use the method in particular environments and situations:

Press the ground with your left foot for 3-4 seconds; relax the muscles and try to perceive the difference between initial tension and subsequent relaxation; repeat 2-3 times; do the same thing with the right foot.

Then move on to the arms, resting on the armrests of

the chair, on a table or on the thighs: press downwards with your left hand for 3-4 seconds; release it and try to perceive, once again, the difference between tension and relaxation; repeat 2-3 times; continue in the same way with the right hand.

The total duration of a session is around 15-20 minutes. In reality the session can be repeated at intervals many times, obtaining a progressive improvement and deepening of relaxation.

It is essential that the tensions that are implemented are progressively greater.

SUBSEQUENT RELAXATION EXERCISES

Learn to see yourself living happily for 15-20 minutes
It's about stimulating the faculties of imagination.

For this reason you just need to find, thanks to the previously explained and practiced muscular relaxation, that level of consciousness between waking and sleeping.

Once you have reached this level, all you need to do is imagine a future situation, that is, an event that will occur in the relatively near future, within two months at most, but it could be a month, a week or even a day.

The situation you are about to imagine must be real, it is

not about dreaming impracticable things but of an event you are about to experience.

Above all, choose something very pleasant: it could be the next weekend with your loved ones, a joyful event, or the next holidays, etc.

Place this situation in a setting that you particularly like: the countryside, the sea, the mountains, or more simply your apartment.

Try to put in and see as many details as you can, the objects, the nature, the atmosphere, the colours.

Choose the time of day you prefer and go there, alone or accompanied by the people you love.

So try to see yourself, perfectly fine, both on a physical and psychological and moral level.

Watch yourself as you move in the chosen frame, trying to see the ground you are walking on, the objects, the colors, the people around you.

In a word, take care of the details of the scene.

Smell the scents, hear the sounds.

Appreciate the state and well-being and harmony that reigns between yourself and everything around you.

After meditating for a moment on this last situation, put the image aside and return to the here and now.

Let yourself fall more deeply right at the edge of sleep and you will be able to appreciate the maximum relaxation of the body, of which you are able to feel even better the regeneration, the state of well being.

You fully experience your calm, your inner peace.

TO RECOVER

When you have finished your exercise, which lasts about twenty minutes, resume your tone of activity, your dynamism, starting with one or two large breaths, allowing yourself to rise to the surface, then moving your feet, hands, face, tensing finally the whole body and stretching.

Do not open your eyes until you are sure that you have completely recovered your level of activity.

This method, simple and fun, has the power to make you see the future, even the most immediate and contingent future, in a positive way.

Revive your motivation.

How many times, in fact, are we conditioned by the negative aspect of the past?

From doubts, from fears?

How many times we have thought:

" *Why bother? Anyway I will never be able to stop being afraid*"

Thanks to the positive image you create, you can also replace a negative image that haunts you, such as FoF, with a positive one such as enjoying a trip and a holiday.

So just don't let yourself be assailed by anxiety, concentrate on your body, relax; at the same time, lower your level of vigilance towards sleep and use this possibility of rich imagination to create the positive.

Let yourself be tempted by the potential of your mind, you will be amazed by the great power of the visualizations.

LEARN TO CHANGE ONE SENSATION WITH ANOTHER ONE

(15-20 minutes.)

We all possess a quite extraordinary, and unfortunately little used, faculty which consists in exchanging one sensation for another.

You can easily experience it, thanks to your training.

Relax, as you usually do, in the sitting position, completely letting go of the muscles of your body, while perceiving, in as much detail as you can, all the sensations that come from it.

Then mentally relax, letting yourself fall with the rhythm of your breathing to that level of consciousness that lies between waking and sleeping.

Then concentrate on a particular perception, easy to experience, such as the heat at the level of one of the hands, heat that you can induce with the specific Autogenic Training exercise explained above.

Once the perception of the heat in your hands is clear, carefully evaluate this sweet, pleasant heat and then imagine it transforming into an equally pleasant freshness.

For example, imagine that a light breeze touches your hand which gradually cools down, that a current of fresh air caresses your hand and concentrate on that progressive cooling of your hand, compared to the other one which it is kept warmer.

After three or four minutes, your hand is pleasantly cool. Then let the initial temperature return little by little.

Evaluate the maximum physical and mental relaxation allowed by this attention that is brought to the exercise and progressively regain all your muscle tone and all your dynamism.

LEARN TO USE YOUR 5 SENSES WELL

(Without time limits)

After total physical and mental relaxation, in the sitting position, try to contemplate yourself *"from the outside"* with ever greater ease, given that your unlimited consciousness has rediscovered all its potential.

To help you further clarify this vision of your body, you can do a simple exercise which consists of deeply inhaling the air while raising your arms and hands above your head, as if you were stretching; hold this inhaled air for a few moments, while contemplating the posture of the body, arms stretched out on the armrests, then exhale very slowly.

After this very simple exercise, relax deeply and meditate on what you have seen and heard, that is to say on the perceptions due to the exercise itself, of a bodily nature, as well as on the precision of your ability to contemplate yourself, an ability that little by little your training will allow you to refine and improve.

You can start the same exercise again once or twice, trying to further clarify your vision of yourself, your attitude, your clothes, but also your inner conscience.

Welcome, in an increasingly elaborate way, all the messages sent by the body, perfecting the concept you have of your body schema.

After having rested by relaxing physically and mentally, after having contemplated your body for the last time, further improve your relaxation, perceiving the messages sent by your legs - following the standing position - of pleasant rest, heat, circulation liberated blood, as well as that regeneration of the whole body, of which you gradually develop all the possibilities, all the capacities.

Thus evaluate the heaviness, the earthly attraction, at the level of your support points.

Now contemplate this body, sitting, still, balanced, at rest, thanks to your unlimited consciousness, which is now able to observe your body, sitting where you are.

Now you will be able to improve those wonderful doors of access to information coming from the outside, which are your senses.

Without these receiving devices, such as smell, taste, sight, hearing and touch, you would not exist at all.

So learn to know them, since they allow you to

communicate with the outside, with your environment, and you will thus improve your possibilities of reaction.

THE SENSE OF SMELL

Start with smell. Your externalized consciousness focuses specifically on the nose, then penetrates along with the air inside the nostrils.

Observe the difference in temperature of this air, which initially, as soon as it enters your nostrils, feels cool, and which then, as it penetrates your nose, progressively warms up.

Smell the odors carried by this air, try to distinguish them.

If possible, if you are exercising outdoors, appreciate the scents of nature; differently you perceive the smells of the place you are in.

You breathe and consider for a few moments this air carrying odors, which your nasal receptors pick up and which are transformed and analyzed by the brain.

Now let yourself sink a little deeper, between waking and sleeping, all impregnated with these smells.

Evaluate, each time more, your state of physical and mental well-being.

THE TASTE

Then concentrate on the mouth, as your consciousness can move within it.

Contemplate the palate, the inside of the cheeks, the dental arches, the teeth themselves, the tongue, carrier of the taste buds, the saliva.

Meditate for a few moments on the taste.

You can take some water that you have placed near you, and savor it.

Fresh water is life. You savor life. You are life.

Rest again by immersing yourself a little more deeply between waking and sleeping.

Measure your sense of well-being again.

ENTERING INTO SYMBIOSIS
WITH THE ENVIRONMENT

Sitting comfortably on your seat, with your back leaning against the backrest, achieve total physical and mental relaxation.

Let yourself go completely to the edge of sleep.

If you have been practicing daily training as recommended, it now only takes you a few minutes to get to this point.

Then contemplate yourself in the place where you are.

Listen to the sounds you hear and appreciate the smells picked up by your sense of smell.

Touch the fabric of your clothing with your fingers; taste your saliva.

Appreciate well these faculties of communication, of communion with your environment.

Meditate on it for a few moments, in silence.

Now sit in an anatomical position, with your back off the chair, perfectly straight.

Close a fist on that lower abdominal point, between the navel and pubis, concentrate on your synchronized breathing with the pressure of your hands.

Leave aside the reality that surrounds you.

Appreciate the complete silence within you, the increase in your vital energy.

SLIDE INTO THE IMMAGINATION

Now imagine a waterfall, try to see it, in its fall and in its colors, in its frame of rocks or greenery, listen to the sound of the water falling on the boulders, the boiling of the water, perceive the freshness that emanates from it, the scent of humidity that spreads.

Try to see yourself, to see yourself near this waterfall, perfectly fine, physically and mentally, appreciate the droplets of water that spray your face, wet your hands in this fresh water, savor it by bringing it to your lips, to your mouth.

What does this imaginary situation make you think of?
What are you doing there? What feeling animates you?
Does your intuition tell you something? Meditate on the
answers that arise spontaneously: they emanate from
the depths of yourselves.

DISCOVER YOUR LIMITAND
YOUR UNIVERSALITY

Sit comfortably again.
Let yourself descend to the edge of sleep.
Appreciate this deepening of your total relaxation.
Listen to the sounds around you, touch your
surroundings again, look at all this; keeping your eyes
closed, savor reality.
The body is there, sitting, motionless, real, limited:
consciousness, for its part, is unlimited, universal.
Meditate on this difference between the real and the
imaginary, on the paradox of your limit and
of your universality.
Deepen your level of vigilance in this superior light, in
this playfulness , in this fertility of active and creative
imagination.
Appreciate the reality that surrounds you, contemplate
your body which you will thus get to know better and
better.

CONTROL THE VITAL ENERGY

Focus your attention on synchronous lower abdominal breathing.

Feel all this mobilized vital energy, which is at your disposal.

Now choose a color, try to materialize it whenever you can during the imaginary situation you visualize.

Imagine taking a walk in a forest.

Try to see yourself on this path, to see the forest, the sun, as you want them to be, as well as your color materialized on the branches of the trees or in the nature that surrounds you.

Appreciate the state of well-being you are in.

Ask yourself the question:

" *What am I doing here?* "

Let the answers come spontaneously.

Meditate as you contemplate yourself on this walk, but to where...?

This type of question always brings with it answers of profound origin, which allows you to get to know yourself better.

Let them come. Meditate on it in the fullness of your silence.

Then sit comfortably again, rest, returning to reality,

integrating yourself again into your environment, whose communication you increasingly appreciate.

You are there, perfectly fine, still in a world that moves around you, a world that you analyze, that you control.

You are this world, you are nature.

AND NOW GET OVER IT

Finally, little by little, you regain your dynamism of activity, realizing this recovery at your own pace and in a complete way.

When you open your eyes, we advise you to write down on a sheet of paper what happened, what you saw and experienced, the answers that presented themselves.

You will thus have the opportunity to reread them and compare them with those that will come as the days pass, depending on your training.

The exercises indicated so far have the advantage of being rather simple and effective, especially if, as we have recommended, they are performed repeatedly starting at least a week or better yet fifteen days before the departure of your plane.

In this way, in times of need, you will have obtained a double result: on the one hand you will have started to reduce your anxiety about the approaching departure (we must never forget that aerophobia is still an anxiety disorder) thus living in a more peaceful manner and peaceful throughout the preparation period, on the other hand you will have acquired a now established " *method* " to reduce your fear until it disappears.

CONCLUSION

If you have read the book up to this point and have started practicing the various techniques illustrated, you are now on the right path.

You have begun to build the tools that will allow you to fly with peace of mind.

But, at the same time, you will have increased your self-knowledge and expanded your awareness which will be useful to you in everyday life, promoting your serenity.

Good flight!

BIBLIOGRAPHICAL REFERENCES

In addition to the exercises illustrated in this book, I believe the meditation techniques linked to Mindfulness and other schools and traditions can be extremely useful.

Below are some of my books that deal with these topics in detail.

1) MEDITAZIONE E MINDFULNESS. COSA È, A COSA SERVE, COME SI PRATICA : COME CURARSI MEDITANDO [5]

2) EFFETTI DELLA MEDITAZIONE MINDFUL SULLA SALUTE : COME CURARSI MEDITANDO Vol.2 [6]

3) MEDITAZIONE MINDFUL. TUTTE LE TECNICHE : Qigong Vipassana Metta Mantra Trascendentale Spirituale Kundalini Zazen Silenziosa Yoga Pranayama Mindfulness [7]

WHO AM I

I am a Nutritionist and a Psychologist.

I have worked for over 30 years in various clinics in Tuscany in the nutrition sector, including with people with Eating Disorders.

I have been a contract professor at the Faculty of Medicine of the University of Pisa and in others.

I continue to carry out online consultations via my website: www.dietazonaonline.com

To find out more about me you can go to my resume/CV https://dietazonaonline.com/curriculum-vitae-dott-buracchi

If you want you can write to me at

g.buracchi@gmail.com

If you are interested in my other books on nutrition, natural health, psychology and novels you can find me on Amazon

https://www.amazon.it/s?=gabriele+buracchi

MY OTHER BOOKS

BIBLIOGRAPHY

---

[1] Panic attacks are episodes of sudden and intense fear or a rapid escalation of normally present anxiety.
They are accompanied by somatic and cognitive symptoms. For example, palpitations, sudden sweating, tremor, feeling of suffocation, chest pain, nausea, dizziness, fear of dying or going crazy, chills or hot flashes.
Those who have experienced panic attacks describe them as a terrible experience, often sudden and unexpected, at least the first time. It is obvious that the fear of a new attack immediately becomes strong and dominant.

[2] https://www.amazon.it/dp/B0CNS4MJFY

[3] https://link.springer.com/article/10.1007/s12646-011-0136-4

[4]   https://openurl.ebsco.com/EPDB%3Agcd%3A16%3A8004352/detailv2?sid=ebsco%3Aplink%3Ascholar&id=ebsco%3Agcd%3A160597886&crl=c

[5] https://www.amazon.it/dp/B0BW7KWM5K

[6] https://www.amazon.it/dp/B0BWJPS371

[7] https://www.amazon.it/dp/B0BWTYJ3F1